WASHOE COUNTY LIBRARY
3 1235 03514 111
D0499136

Colorful Peacocks

by Deborah Underwood

No Longer Property Of
Washoe County Library

Lerner Publications Company • Minneapolis

For John

Text copyright ©2007 by Deborah Underwood

All rights reserved. International copyright secured. No part of this book may be reproduced, stored in a retrieval system, or transmitted in any form or by any means—electronic, mechanical, photocopying, recording, or otherwise—without the prior written permission of Lerner Publishing Group, Inc., except for the inclusion of brief quotations in an acknowledged review.

Lerner Publications Company
A division of Lerner Publishing Group, Inc.
241 First Avenue North
Minneapolis, MN 55401 U.S.A.

Website address: www.lernerbooks.com

Words in *italic* type are explained in a glossary on page 30.

Library of Congress Cataloging-in-Publication Data

Underwood, Deborah.
Peacocks / by Deborah Underwood.
p. cm. — (Pull ahead books)
ISBN-13: 978-0-8225-5930-6 (lib. bdg. : alk. paper)
ISBN-10: 0-8225-5930-7 (lib. bdg. : alk. paper)
1. Peafowl—Juvenile literature. I. Title. II. Series.
QL696.G27U53 2007
598.6'17—dc22 2005017977

Manufactured in the United States of America
3 4 5 6 7 8 — JR — 14 13 12 11 10 09

Look at this bird's beautiful feathers!

What kind of bird is it?

This bird is a peacock. Long *train feathers* trail behind a peacock.

Look at the spot at the end of a train feather. The spot is called an *eyespot*.

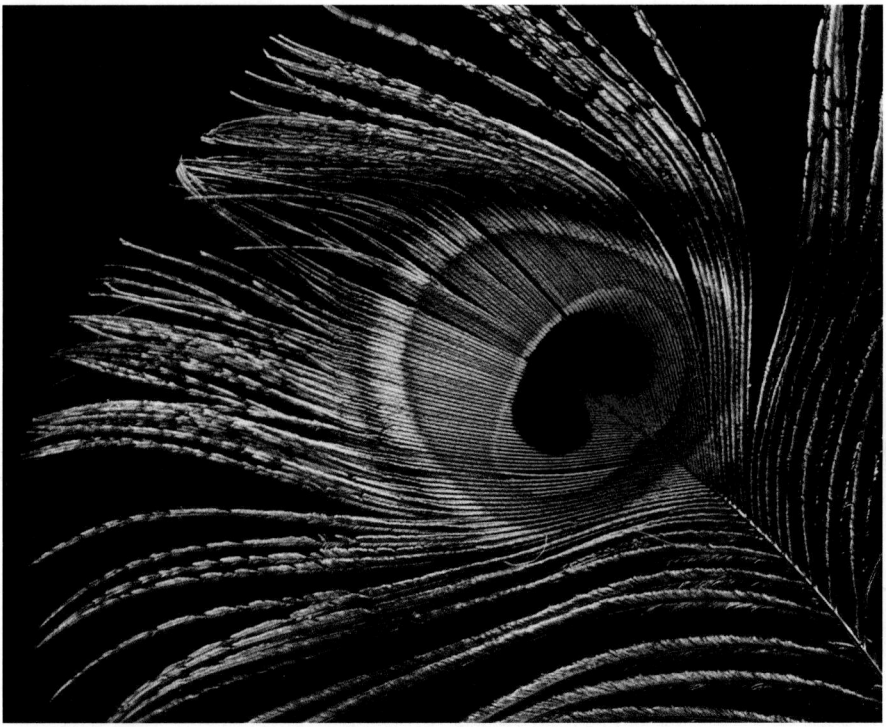

Can you see why?

Whoosh! This peacock lifts his train feathers to make a beautiful fan.

Look behind this peacock's fan.

Can you see the peacock's short tail feathers?

All peacocks are male.

They have bright blue heads and necks.

Females are called *peahens*.

Peahens are not as colorful as peacocks.

But peahens can fly better than peacocks. They do not have long train feathers to slow them down.

Together, peacocks and peahens are called *peafowl*.

Each peafowl has a *crest* on its head. A crest is a crown of feathers.

Peafowl live in parks and gardens.

Peafowl can live where it is very hot.

They can also live where it is very cold.

During the day, peafowl stay on the ground.

At night, they *roost* in trees. They rest on the branches of trees.

A peacock's feathers blend in with the trees.

This helps a peacock hide from enemies.

Can you find a peacock in this tree?

Peafowl eat insects, grains, fruits, seeds, and flowers.

Sometimes they eat frogs or snakes.
They drink from ponds or streams.

This peahen is about to lay eggs.
This piece of ground is her nest.

A peahen usually lays five to eight eggs.

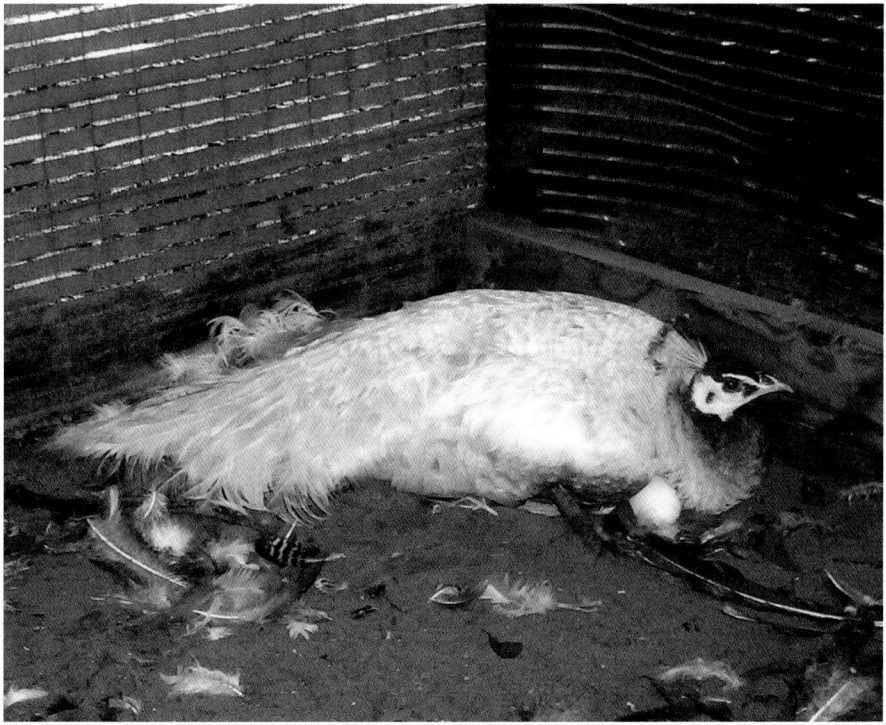

She sits on the eggs to keep them warm.

Four weeks after the eggs are laid, the baby birds *hatch*.

Baby peafowl are called *peachicks*. The peachicks have fuzzy feathers.

Peachicks can stand soon after they hatch.

Their mother helps them find food.

Peachicks stay near their mother. The peachicks can't fly. At night, they stay on the ground with their mother.

Male peachicks don't have train feathers. Those feathers grow when a peacock is three years old.

Then the peacock can make a feather fan. Whoosh! He is all grown up.

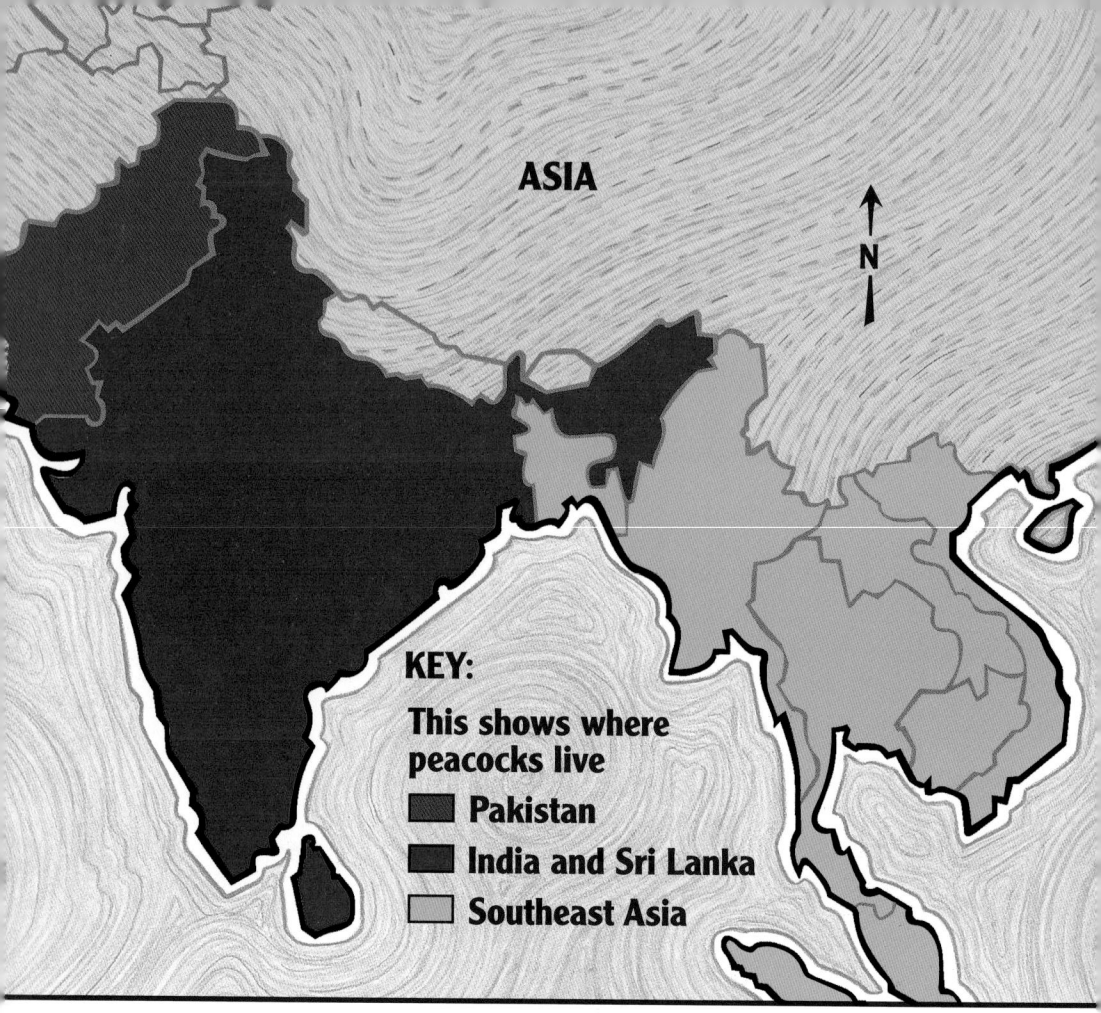

This is a map of Asia.
Where do peacocks live?

Parts of a Peacock's Body

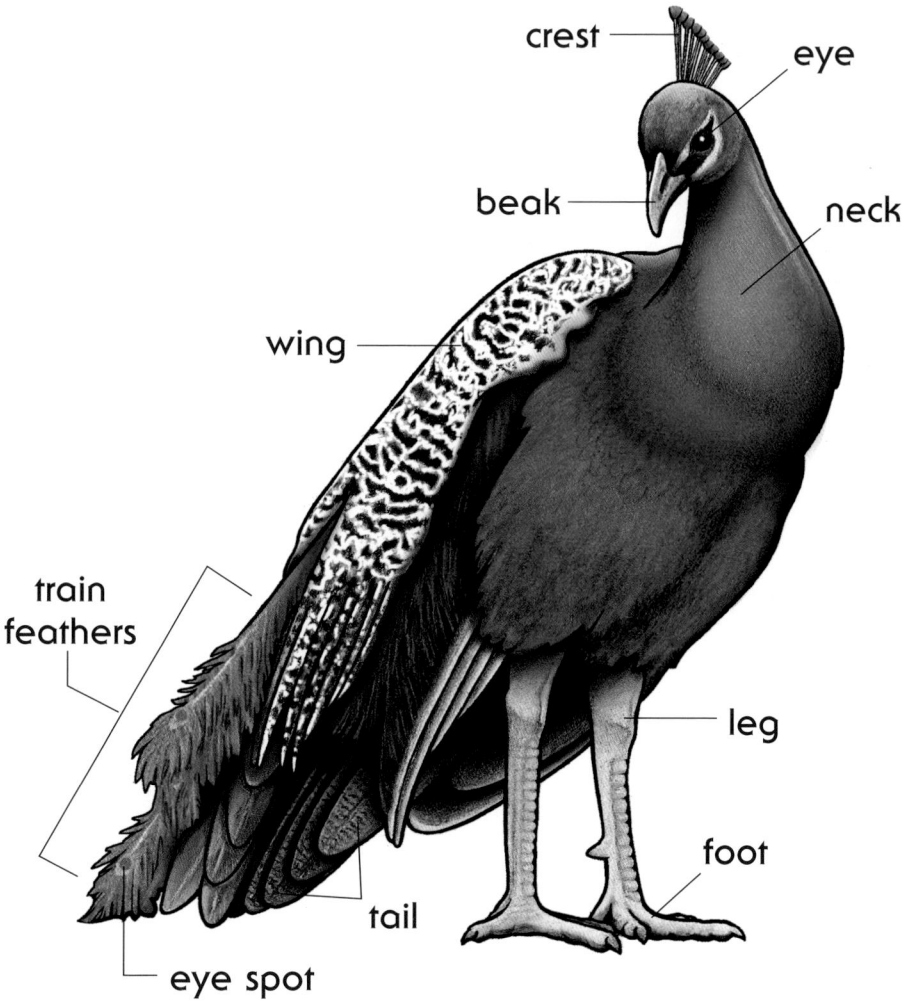

Glossary

crest: a crown of feathers on a peafowl's head

eyespot: a spot at the end of a peacock's train feathers

hatch: to come out of the egg

peachicks: baby peacocks and peahens

peafowl: the name for peacocks, peahens, and peachicks as a group

peahens: female peafowl

roost: to rest or sleep in the branches of a tree

train feathers: the long feathers that make a peacock's fan

Further Reading and Websites

Donaldson, Madeline. *Asia*. Minneapolis: Lerner Publications Company, 2005.

Animal Facts
http://wildwnc.org/af/peafowl.html

Enchanted Learning: All about Birds
http://www.enchantedlearning.com/subject/birds

Index

eating, 18–19, 24

eggs, 20–21

fan, 6–7, 27

feathers, 3–7, 10, 11, 16, 22, 26–27

flying, 10

roosting, 15

standing, 23

Photo Acknowledgments

The photographs in this book are reproduced with the permission of: © Dr. John D. Cunningham/Visuals Unlimited, front cover; © James P. Rowan, pp. 3, 10; © Allan Friedlander/SuperStock, pp. 4, 31; PhotoDisc Royalty Free by Getty Images, pp. 5, 27; © Glenn Oliver/Visuals Unlimited, p. 6; © Adam Jones/Visuals Unlimited, pp. 7, 8; © Carol Cook, www.peacockemporium.net, pp. 9, 18, 21, 22; © Michael H. Francis, pp. 11, 13; © Charles Fredeen, p. 12; © William Weber/Visuals Unlimited, p. 14; © Art Wolfe, p. 15; © Jerry Amster/SuperStock, p. 16; © Krupakar Senani/Oxford Scientific Films, p. 17; © Gerald Cubitt, p. 19; © Hopkins' Alternative Livestock, pp. 20, 26; © Mary C. Kauffman, pp. 23, 24; © Dr. Carleton Ray/Photo Researchers, Inc., p. 25.